# ROLLING STONES

## LEGENDS ALPHABET

Words by Robin Feiner

**A** is for **A**ngie.
This legendary, wistful ballad is all about being stuck in the throes of heartache. With no lovin' in their souls and no money in their coats, the Stones showed how tough it can be to say goodbye to a former flame. They left fans forever asking, 'Angie! When will those clouds all disappear?'

**B** is for **B**east of Burden. After a stint away from the band, guitarist Keith Richards returned with this slow-rocking hit, which featured on their Some Girls album. His legendary lyrics work in two ways—as a thank you to Mick Jagger for shouldering the burden of Richards' absence and for all the pretty, pretty, pretty girls.

**C is for Fool to Cry.
This deep cut sees the
legendary Stones frontman,
Mick Jagger, taking a hard
look in the mirror. He's so,
so down on himself and only
his loving daughter and wife
can bring back his joy. Over
and over, in piercing falsettos,
they tell a down-and-out
Jagger, 'Daddy, you're
a fool to cry!'**

**D** is for Tumbling **D**ice. 'Got to roll me, yeah!' The lead single on Exile on Main St. sees the Stones at their funky best. It's a wonder of unorthodox tempo, but more than anything, it shows how dedicated they were to greatness—they did more than 150 takes to record the perfect version of this song!

"EMOTIONAL RESCUE"

**E** is for **E**motional Rescue. Jagger sure could hit those falsetto notes, and nowhere is that truer than on this tune from the Stones' legendary 1980 album of the same name. In his singular high-pitched cries, Mick pleads for his girl to come back, all while taking the band in a new disco-focused direction.

**F** is for Play With **F**ire. She might have her diamonds, and she might have her fancy clothes— but the Stones never saw wealth as a reason to treat people differently! With tough-nosed lyrics and a tambourine in hand, legendary Mick Jagger burnt that message into the souls of their listeners.

G is for Gimme Shelter. This searing tune shows the Stones at their most innovative. It's a politically-minded masterpiece, a reminder that a threatening storm is always just a kiss away. Oh, and give it up for Merry Clayton's earth-shattering vocals: 'It's just a shot away, shot away, yeah!'

**H** is for **H**onky Tonk Women. With its distinctive opening cowbell and the slicing guitar riffs that follow, Honky Tonk Women is an ode to women who love to dance. It's for the girls who love rock 'n' roll, the girls who love the blues, and the girls who love to strut in leather boots and cowboy hats!

I is for (I Can't Get No) Satisfaction. This legendary anti-establishment bop starts with a guitar riff that strikes like lightning and ends with the catchiest hook of all time. Whether driving in a car or watching TV, the Stones won't let the man tell them what to do. Cause they can't get no... oh no, no, no!

**J** is for **J**umpin' Jack Flash. There are those of us born in crossfire hurricanes and those who can't help but frown at the crumbs of life. But this exhilarating, legendary tune reminds listeners that it's possible to break free from all those hard times. As Mick says: 'It's alright now, in fact, it's a gas!'

K is for Can't You Hear Me Knocking. You've got to give it up for the Stones' instrumental creativity. On this rocking classic, they were free-jamming to their hearts' content, unaware that a recording was still in session. But luckily, the tapes were running, the material was brilliant, and an all-timer was captured.

**L** is for **L**et's Spend the Night Together. Released as a 1967 single, this legendary bop became so popular that one of the Stones' original rock mentors, Muddy Waters, eventually recorded a cover of it. The message is clear: whether you're with your best friend or a crush, there's joy in spending the night together!

**M** is for Start **M**e Up. 'We'll never stop, never, never, never stop!' Though originally recorded in 1978, Start Me Up was finished and released as a massive single three years later. Fitting for the Stones' drive and dedication, it went on to become an anthem in sports stadiums around the world!

**N** is for **19th Nervous Breakdown.** The inspiration behind this legendary track about losing your patience came from a grueling, months-long tour in 1965 after Jagger had run out of steam. He said to his fellow band members: 'Blokes, I feel about ready for my 19th nervous breakdown!'

**O is for Time Is On My Side.** There's nothing worse than heartache. But our true love, the one we're meant for, they'll always come running back, right? The Stones made that clear on this tambourine-filled, tender ballad, which they first performed to love-struck teens on the Ed Sullivan Show in 1964.

**Pp**

is for    aint It Black.
Capturing the era of the
Vietnam War, this tune about
a loss of innocence was
inspired by the loss of a lover.
This legendary track—from
the Aftermath album—is laden
with experimental Middle
Eastern sounds and became
one of the Stones' biggest
chart toppers.

**Q** is for Little **Q**ueenie. The Stones played this at many concerts as an ode to the Father of Rock and Roll, Chuck Berry. It's a bluesy anthem dedicated to a bride-to-be. Little Queenie is so stunning and put together that her soon-to-be hubby has weak knees and a lump in his throat!

R is for She's A Rainbow.
'She shoots colors all around,
like a sunset going down.
Have you seen her?' With
vibrant tones and mystical
imagery, She's a Rainbow
is a guaranteed good time.
It's the Stones at their most
joyous—a legendary song
written for Marianne Faithfull,
Jagger's greatest love.

**S** is for **S**ympathy for the Devil. Who's the angry singer of this legendary, bongo-touting track? Well, it's none other than the devil himself. Or is it? According to Jagger, the legendary lyrics are also meant to confront the darkness within us all. 'Pleased to meet you! Hope you've guessed my name! Oh yeah!'

T is for Ruby Tuesday.
Richards and Jagger were known for their tales of heartbreak and longing. This legendary, catchy tune is one of their best—it blends mourning for yesterday with optimism for tomorrow. As for the mysterious Ruby? 'Who could ever say where she came from?'

U is for Under My Thumb. This 1966 single about a power struggle in a relationship was a breakout on the band's wildly experimental Aftermath album. Multi-instrumental legend Brian Jones put the marimbas to use while Mick sang of a lover who once had him under her thumb—but now the change has come!

**V** is for Love in **V**ain.
On the way to the station, with their suitcase in hand and the train rolling down the tracks, the Stones injected a country vibe into Robert Johnson's classic tune, Love in Vain Blues. It's a tear-jerking song about a man who's lost his lady and, sadly, all his love was in vain.

**W is for Wild Horses.**
**A message to Keith Richards'**
**son? Or a love letter to**
**Mick Jagger's lost lover?**
**While the debate rages on,**
**the emotional weight of**
**this tender ballad is never**
**in doubt. The Stones love**
**someone dearly, and nothing,**
**nothing, can drag them**
**away, not even wild horses.**

**X** is for **E**xile on Main St. There's an ode to a former lover, notes about the wild ride of relationships, and tender moments where the band reminisces over Brian Jones after his passing. Add it all up, and it's no wonder experts call Exile on Main St. the Stones' greatest album, and one of the best rock albums ever recorded.

**Y** is for **Y**ou Can't Always Get What You Want. This legendary track, with a heavenly intro featuring a chorus of choir boys, is about the importance of waiting for happiness. It can be hard and even seem impossible, but if you try sometimes, well, you just might find, you get what you need!

**Z** is for Back to **Z**ero. Hidden on the Dirty Work album is this 1980s gem. It's a new wave track from a band in transition, a story about refusing to lose. The Stones did whatever they could—including experimenting with new sounds—to maintain their legendary success and avoid going Back to Zero.

# The ever-expanding legendary library

**EXPLORE THESE LEGENDARY ALPHABETS & MORE AT WWW.ALPHABETLEGENDS.COM**

**ROLLING STONES LEGENDS ALPHABET**
www.alphabetlegends.com

Published by Alphabet Legends Pty Ltd in 2023
Created by Beck Feiner
Copyright © Alphabet Legends Pty Ltd 2023

Printed and bound in China.

9780645851458

**ALPHABET LEGENDS**